SURVIVING
IN
SYMBOLS

Surviving
in
Symbols

A Visit to the
Pictish Nation

Martin Carver

Series editor: Gordon Barclay

CANONGATE BOOKS
with
HISTORIC SCOTLAND

THE MAKING OF SCOTLAND

Series editor:
Gordon Barclay

Other titles available:

WILD HARVESTERS:
The First People in Scotland

FARMERS, TEMPLES AND TOMBS:
Scotland in the Neolithic and Early Bronze Age

SETTLEMENT AND SACRIFICE:
The Later Prehistoric People of Scotland

A GATHERING OF EAGLES:
Scenes from Roman Scotland

THE SEA ROAD:
A Viking Voyage through Scotland

SAINTS AND SEA-KINGS:
The First Kingdom of the Scots

ANGELS, FOOLS AND TYRANTS:
Britons and Anglo-Saxons in Southern Scotland AD 450–750

First published in Great Britain in 1999
by Canongate Books Ltd, 14 High Street,
Edinburgh EH1 1TE

Text copyright © Martin Carver 1999
Illustrations © individuals and organisations as credited
Maps © Rob Burns

British Library Cataloguing-in-Publication Data
A catalogue record for this book is available on request
from the British Library

ISBN 0 86241 876 3

Series Design:
James Hutcheson, Canongate Books

Design by:
Alistair Hodge

Printed and bound by
Mateu Cromo, Spain

Previous page
A panorama of Nechtansmere, scene of a crucial battle in 685,
when the Pictish forces defeated those of Northumbria
and put an end to Anglian expansion northwards.

Contents

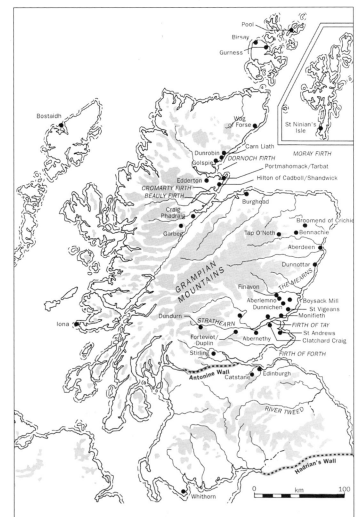

Location Map
Places mentioned
in the text.

Carving a Symbol Stone

An imaginary scene by the shores of the Dornoch Firth in the spring of AD 640. Pictish sculptors expressed ideas in symbols, some in the form of expertly drawn animals, others with distinctive and suggestive but unidentified shapes. The symbols occur all over the eastern part of Scotland and resemble each other closely, so probably relied on a small group of specialists, who travelled about, in the manner of celebrated pipers. They may have carried their patterns in their heads, But here we speculate that some images at least were carried on their bodies, by one of the very oldest forms of picture-making – tattooing with natural dyes. Dyes, or red clay or charcoal were also probably used to bring out the pattern once it had been incised onto the stone. The models for the stones are, foreground, from the Brough of Birsay, Orkney, and in the middle distance, Dunrobin 1, Sutherland.

MIKE MOORE

A Preliminary Gallop

In this book we pay a visit to the Picts, an artistically brilliant people who occupied the eastern part of north Britain around AD 300 to 900, but who then lost their identity and were largely forgotten. Who were they? What did they believe in? What became of them?

The little that was written down about the Picts is owed to authors in neighbouring lands, particularly to the Northumbrian historian Bede of Jarrow and Adomnán of Iona, the biographer of St Columba. Although the Picts left no history of their own, it can be seen from their archaeology that they were a nation of great warriors and artists, who farmed, hunted, defended their territory and set up stone monuments carved with people, animals and symbols. The meaning of the symbols, so elegant and enigmatic, is unknown but they were possibly used to mark territory and make statements about identity and belief. They survive as signposts to show us where 'Pictland' was and urge us to rediscover its people's special contribution to the history of what is now Scotland.

The people nicknamed *Picti* by the Romans patrolling Hadrian's Wall lived in extended settlements with underground stores (the 'souterrains') and buried their dead in stone-lined graves under mounds of earth or cairns of stones. Even though they were not incorporated within the Roman province of Britannia, they were in contact with it, and occasionally provoked Emperors into making punitive campaigns against them. In the 300s, as Roman control weakened, Picts raided more extensively across the Wall, sometimes in league with the *Scotti* or Scots, their neighbours to the west. By the 400s, Roman Imperial control had officially ceased, and Britain, largely a Romanised Christian island, was trying to resist takeover by pagan Germanic peoples from north Germany. It

was at this time that the southern Picts were probably visited by a British missionary, St Ninian of Whithorn, although there is little evidence for a lasting conversion. In the 500s, the northern Picts were evangelised by St Columba, founder of the Scottish monastery on Iona, whose mission may have resulted in some localised Christian communities, but probably not in the conversion of the leaders, or of the people as a whole. During his visit of AD 565, St Columba met one of the first great figures of Pictish history, Bridei son of Mailchon, who, from a base near Inverness, claimed control of a large territory spreading from Skye to Orkney. By this time, the Pictish people had begun to fortify coastal promontories (as at Burghead) or rocky outcrops (as at Dundurn), and to mark their burials or their territory with symbols carved on unshaped stones standing in the landscape.

In the early 600s, the Germanic incomers (Angles), who had been building up a kingdom in Northumbria, began to expand to west and north, and their pagan king Aethelfrith (593–617) undertook ruthless campaigns against the Scots and Britons. His successor, Edwin, also a warlike ruler, accepted Christianity in 627 and aligned with the southern English and with the Church of Rome. During Edwin's reign the disinherited sons of Aethelfrith – Eanfrith, Oswiu and Oswald – were given asylum by the Scots and the Picts, Oswald becoming a Scottish Christian and Eanfrith marrying into the Pictish aristocracy. These events had a significant effect on the subsequent history of all the peoples of the north. Under Oswald (634–641) Northumbria sided ideologically with Iona but, after the Synod of Whitby in 664, it realigned towards Rome and southern England, and began forcibly spreading the message of the Roman–English union.

Potted Picts – a timeline

PEOPLE	PLACES	OBJECTS
300–600		
297 'Picti' mentioned by Eumenius	By 500: Roundhouses with underground stores (**Newmill**)	400s–700s: **Class I symbol stones** (**Dunrobin, Easterton of Roseisle, Bransdbutt, Dunnichen, Birsay, Crichie**)
367 **Picts** and Scots overrun Hadrian's Wall	By 600: forts constructed (**Burghead, Dundurn, Clatchard Craig**); **Portmahomack** occupied	Painted pebbles
Late 400s: St Ninian at Whithorn; missions to the southern **Picts**	Cemeteries of square-ditched burial mounds (**Garbeg, Whitebridge, Boysack Mill**)	Double-sided combs
c.560 **Picts** defeat Scots in Dál Riata	c.450–550: Early Christian cemeteries in Galloway (Whithorn), Lothian, Angus and Fife	500s–600s: disc-headed pins, chains and bracelets (**Gaulcross, Whitecleugh**)
563–597 St Columba in Iona; missions to northern **Picts**		
565–585 **Bridei son of Mailchon king of Picts**		
600–700		
617–633 Edwin king in Northumbria; 627 Northumbria converted	634 Oswald erects a wooden cross before the victory at Heavenfield	600s: **Norrie's Law plaques**
	672 **Pictish** army massacred by Ecgfrith of Northumbria	'E-ware' reaches **Craig Phadraig** and **Clatchard Craig** from France
664 Synod of Whitby: Northumbria aligns with Roman Christians	673 Maelrubai founds Applecross	
672–693 Bridei son of Bili king of Picts	681 **Dunnottar** (?) and **Dundurn** under attack	Birsay disc
		680 Book of Durrow illuminated on Iona
679–704 Adomnán abbot of Iona, writing his *Life of St Columba*	685 Battle of **Nechtansmere** (**Dunnichen Moss**). **Picts** defeat Angles and kill Ecgfrith of Northumbria	
700–800		
c.706–724 **Nechtan son of Derile king of Picts**	600s–800s: cellular houses in the western and northern isles (**Buckquoy, Birsay, Pool, Bostaidh**). Round-ended houses in Pictland (**Pitcarmick, Wag of Forse**)	c. 700 The Lindisfarne Gospels
710 Ceolfrith of Jarrow writes to **Nechtan**. **Picts** align with Northumbrian Christians		
717 Columban clergy expelled by **Nechtan**	600s–800s: long-cist graves in Pictland (**The Hallow Hill, St Andrews**)	700s–800s: **Class II stone monuments**
729–761 **Angus I son of Fergus king of Picts**. New ecclesiastical foundation at **St Andrews**		
731 Bede's *History of the English Church and People* completed	793–795 First Viking raids on Lindisfarne and Iona	late 700s **St Andrews Sarcophagus** made (perhaps to bury Nechtan or Angus I)
789 **Constantine son of Fergus king of Picts**		780–810 Book of Kells begun on Iona
800–850		
c.811–820 Constantine son of Fergus king of **Picts** and Scots. New ecclesiastical foundation at **Dunkeld**	c.800 Norse settlement in Shetland, Orkney, Caithness	c.800 **St Ninian's Isle treasure**; penannular brooches (**Blair Atholl, Dunkeld**)
	807 Iona community removes to Kells	
820–834 **Angus II son of Fergus king of Picts** and Scots.	839 Major Viking victory over the **Picts**	c.800 **Tarbat, Nigg, Shandwick, Hilton of Cadboll** stone monuments
840s Kenneth son of Alpin king of Scots and **Picts**	Pictish leaders based at **Forteviot**	
849 Relics of St Columba installed in southern **Pictland**	**Dundurn, Clatchard Craig, Burghead** abandoned	Burghead blast-horn
875 Halfdan attacks **Picts** and Strathclyde Britons	Danes attack Norse in the Isles. Some Norse migrate to Iceland	c.820 **Dupplin Cross** dedicated to Constantine son of Fergus
895 Turf Einarr, Earl of Orkney		c.900 Sueno's stone

Pictish people, places and objects in bold

From 670 Ecgfrith, the new king of Northumbria, began to campaign against Pictland, which was perhaps still largely pagan at that date. But Anglian expansion northwards was brought to a halt when he was killed and his army massacred by Bridei son of Bili at the Battle of Nechtansmere in 685.

In the early 700s, king Nechtan son of Derile decided to explore a Christian alliance with Northumbria and sent to Jarrow for information about its church. In the power centres of Tayside and the Moray Firth, a new model of monument appeared, carrying the cross as well as Pictish symbols carved in relief on rectangular upright slabs. But from the mid 700s, Nechtan's successor, the great Angus son of Fergus, again turned the Picts towards the west and the Scottish families of Dál Riata, the Scottish kingdom in the Argyll area. From then on the Pictish–Scottish alliance grew until little distinction could be drawn between the two peoples. In the early 800s, Constantine and Angus II, kings of both Picts and Scots, were supporting major ecclesiastical centres at Dunkeld and St Andrews, and cherishing the relics of St

Columba. The new political players on the scene were now the Norse from Norway, raiding and settling in the Northern and Western Isles and coastlands. But in the old Pictish mainland, south of the Moray Firth, the Norse either never succeeded in settling or were soon absorbed.

Judging from their material culture, the Picts were a nation of individual leaders, male and female, who had access to tracts of land and the resources to put up stone memorials. Collectively they had escaped incorporation into the Roman empire, resisted English encroachment and seemed to have been unenthusiastic about the medieval political formula of a single dynastic king supported by the Christian network. When it came, the formula was delivered by their neighbours, and the people of eastern Scotland lost their separate identity. In so far as the Picts had a united view of the world, it survives in their symbols.

Britons, Angles, Scots, Norse – Christians from the west and the south, pagans from the south and the north – during their days on the international stage, the Pictish nation had plenty to cope with and to confront through diplomacy, debate, war, art or marriage. The subsequent centuries have not been kind to the Picts, and have buried them in the shifting sands of undated archaeology or under the tangled vegetation of myth and legend. But, of all the peoples who made Scotland, none had such deep roots in the prehistory of the land or left so individual a legacy. It is a legacy into which modern scholars are now energetically inquiring.

Merger at Dunfallandy, Perthsire, about AD 800

Two seated figures, apparently clerics with thrown back hoods, face each other over a cross. Above them hover the ancestral symbols of the Picts: the Pictish beast, the crescent and V-rod, the double disc. The double disc is also used to 'label' clerics at Logierait and St Vigeans.
HISTORIC SCOTLAND

The Stone at Broomend of Crichie, Aberdeenshire

This stone is now placed within a much earlier religious site.

RCAHMS

Out of Prehistory

Backs to the mountains, faces to the sea

Scotland, land of lochs, mountains, moorland, forests and fields, offers many different kinds of terrain for settlers. To the south are rolling hills of rich pasture, drained by clear shallow rivers such as the Tweed. To the west, the high land drops steeply to the Irish Sea, providing a landscape of old smooth rocks and turf, with many thousands of islands. To the east, the weather is drier and there are great areas of fertile arable land, located in coastal enclaves that are almost countries of their own: Fife, the Mearns, Strathearn, the Aberdeenshire plain, the Moray Laigh, Tarbat Ness, the Golspie strip. In contrast to the west, there are few islands, but the coast is cut by three great groups of estuaries, now called by their Scandinavian name, 'firth' (equivalent to the Norse *fjord*). In the north-east, the good land clusters round the Moray Firth, with its neighbours the Dornoch, Cromarty and Beauly Firths. Together these make up a fertile coastline hundreds of miles long, with farms and estates in view of each other and in reach by boat. In the south, the Firth of Tay is flanked by more productive land still, in Angus (and Fife), and further inland by the arable and pasture lands of Strathearn. The Firth of Forth provides a southern border.

Blocking the centre of Scotland lies the mountain range of the Grampians, and the *Druim Alban* ('the spine of Britain') which defines and separates the lands of east and west. In the days before roads and railways, these hills presented a formidable barrier, crossed or avoided by three principal routes: by boat around the north coast; along the ancient routeway of the Great Glen, which by horse and boat connected the Inverness area with Argyll; or across the lowlands between Edinburgh, Glasgow and the Stirling gap – a crossroads where the peoples of the highlands and the lowlands and the North Sea and the Irish Sea have encountered each other over the centuries. In general terms, the natural regions of the Scottish peninsula also made homes for separate peoples: the Scots to the west, the Britons to the south, and the Picts to the east.

Deep roots

The eastern part of Scotland, called here 'Pictland', has had a distinctive material culture over thousands of years, the Pictish culture being only the latest we see. One of the earliest markers of this territory was the *carved stone ball*, an enigmatic artefact, Neolithic or early Bronze Age in date (*Farmers, Temples and Tombs*, p. 40). In the early Iron Age, a particular type of hill-fort was built. Dated to about 600–300 BC, these hill-forts had rubble ramparts laced with timbers which were later burnt – producing such a high temperature that the

The Provinces of the northern Picts . . . are separated from those of the southern Picts by a range of steep and desolate mountains.

Bede of Jarrow

The Venerable Bede, England's first historian, lived most of his life at a monastery at Jarrow on Tyneside, and died there in AD 735. His writing, especially his great work *A History of the English Church and People*, contains some legends about Pictish origins, but also offers us first-hand testimony of the Picts as he saw them. Bede, being Northumbrian, had his own partisan views about his neighbours to the north.

> *The population of Pictland and the Irish who lived in Britain, [were] races separated by the mountains of Druim Alban.*
>
> Adomnán of Iona

Adomnán of Iona wrote an adulatory account of the work and miracles of his famous predecessor St Columba. The Life of St Columba contains a number of important contemporary observations on the northern Picts. Adomnán died in 704; Bede called him 'a good and wise man with excellent knowledge of the scriptures'.

The Vitrified Fort at Finavon, Angus
Constructed during the first millennium BC, these important Iron Age centres occupied good defensive positions, as here, and overlooked extensive areas of land. Other famous Iron Age forts include Abernethy (Perth), Monifieth (Angus), and Craig Phadraig, all of which were to have a later association with the Picts.
RCAHMS

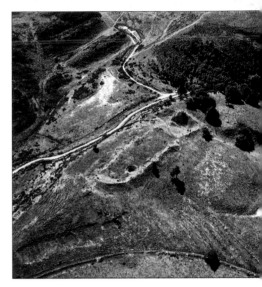

rubble fused into a glassy mass, from which they are called *vitrified forts.* Also within our region is a group of settlements consisting of circular buildings in turf or timber, with a very distinctive type of underground store: the *souterrain* (*Settlement and Sacrifice*, pp. 38–9). Souterrains were certainly used throughout the eastern territory and, although most excavated examples date from before AD 200, they may have remained in use for longer.

(*left*)
Roundhouses and Souterrains
At Newmills, near Bankfoot, Perthshire, a large roundhouse about 17.6m in diameter seems to have had a souterrain to itself. The people who lived on these sites were contemporaries of the Romans manning Hadrian's Wall, and had access to Roman objects, such as glass and brooches, although they were not part of a Roman province. The large house at Newmill, the latest in a sequence there, hints at an increase in social status.
HISTORIC SCOTLAND

(*left*)
The Broch at Gurness, Orkney
Brochs were constructed in the north and west during the Roman Iron Age (first century BC to first century AD), but at some sites occupation continued well into the Pictish period (200s to 800s). Here at Gurness, a Pictish group of cellular buildings was found outside the broch.
M.O.H. CARVER

On the Atlantic coasts of the north and west, there appeared in later prehistoric times a series of circular stone structures: the impenetrable tall *brochs* with their 'cooling tower' shape, and the partially underground *wheel-houses* with their radial walls inside. Such 'Atlantic' buildings continued to develop in the Dark Ages, into figure-of-eight and cellular plans; and although all the examples so far come from the Northern or Western Isles, beyond the Pictish heartland, some of them were probably adopted or adapted by the makers of the symbol stones. So, if these stones are now the main surviving markers of Pictish territory, it was a territory with roots deep in prehistory.

Prehistory of Pictland

Distribution of vitrified forts (Iron Age centres dating to the mid first millennium BC), souterrains (underground stores dating to the period 200 BC–AD 200) and brochs (fortified dwellings of the period first century BC to first century AD). The area which was to become Pictland had a number of prehistoric peoples in the same area; it is also the best arable land in Scotland.

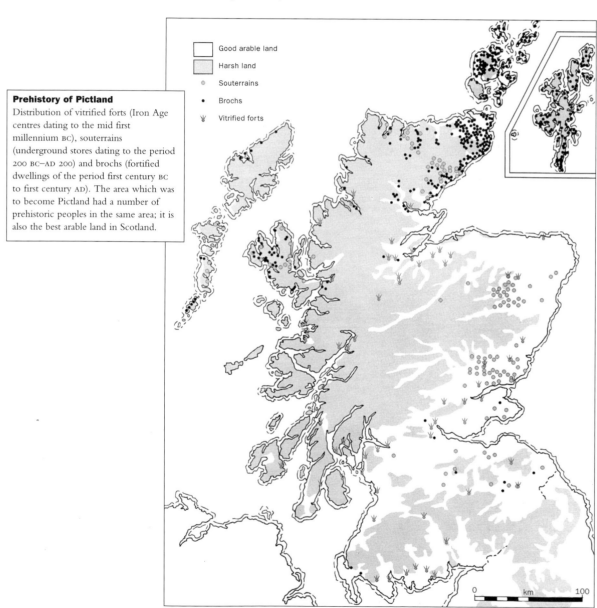

Good arable land
Harsh land
Souterrains
Brochs
Vitrified forts

According to the Neighbours . . .

Calling people names

In the first century AD the Romans called Scotland 'Caledonia' – and advanced into the eastern part of it on a mission of conquest under Agricola, the Provincial Governor. In AD 82, somewhere north of the Forth, the Ninth Legion was surprised and nearly lost in a night attack. A year later at *Mons Graupius* (perhaps Bennachie in Aberdeenshire) the Romans confronted a massed gathering of Caledonians under their leader, the heroic Calgacus, and defeated them. A Roman fleet sailed round the north of Britain in a victory tour, but later emperors decided to leave the region out of the Province of Britannia, establishing the boundary first at Hadrian's Wall, then at the Antonine Wall between the Forth and Clyde, and finally at Hadrian's Wall again. The people beyond the walls were known at first by typical British tribal names – Venicones, Decantae, Cornavii – but by the 300s they had acquired a nickname: the Picts or 'the Painted People'. Giving nicknames was a widespread Dark Age habit: the 'Saxons' seem to have been named after the knives they carried and the 'Vikings' after their habit of dodging in and out of creeks.

During the first millennium AD, at least five peoples competed for territory in the land that was to become Scotland: the Britons (in Strathclyde and the southern lowlands), the Scots (in the west, the territory they called Dál Riata), the Angles (in Lothian and Tweeddale), the Picts (in the east) and, from the 800s onwards, if not before, the Scandinavians (in the far north and the west, along the 'sea road'). These peoples spoke different languages, and generally believed in different ways of living, of governing people and controlling land. Over several centuries there was a long-running debate between shifting factions, occasionally breaking into war. Ruined and defunct, but ever lingering in people's minds, was another silent contestant, the mighty ghost of the Roman Empire, a model to which every great British and European leader then, and later, was drawn. In the fourth to the ninth century, that Empire was being reborn as Christianity. These centuries, the time of the Picts, were once known as the Dark Ages because so little was known about them; now they are called the Early Medieval period or (in Scotland) the Early Historic period, a period illuminated both by documents and by archaeology.

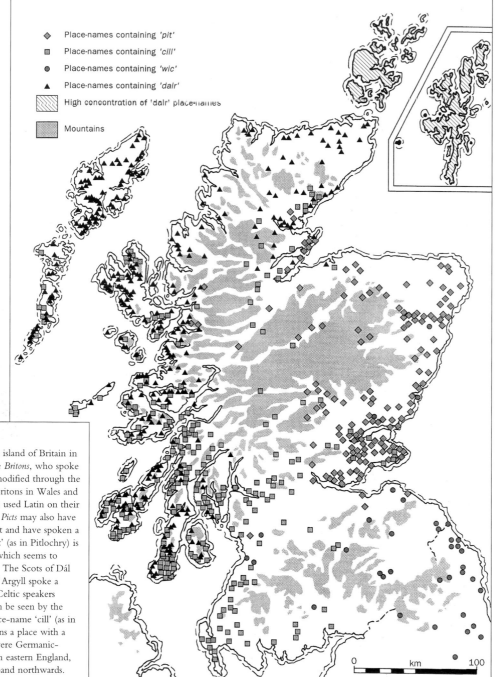

The legend reads:

◆ Place-names containing *'pit'*
■ Place-names containing *'cill'*
● Place-names containing *'wic'*
▲ Place-names containing *'dalr'*
▨ High concentration of 'dalr' place-names
▦ Mountains

0   km   100

Naming the Land

The inhabitants of the island of Britain in the Iron Age were the *Britons*, who spoke a p-Celtic language, modified through the Roman occupation. Britons in Wales and southern Scotland also used Latin on their memorial stones. The *Picts* may also have been of British descent and have spoken a p-Celtic language. 'Pit' (as in Pitlochry) is a Pictish place-name which seems to mean a farm or estate. The Scots of Dál Riata in the region of Argyll spoke a q-Celtic language; q-Celtic speakers spread eastwards as can be seen by the distribution of the place-name 'cill' (as in Kilmartin) which means a place with a church. The Angles were Germanic-speakers who settled in eastern England, but soon began to expand northwards. Some of their settlements are called 'wic' (as in Berwick), a market or place of exchange. The *Norse*, also Germanic-speakers, were later on the scene. 'Dalr' (valley) (as in Helmsdale) was a name given to their district centres. On this distribution, the Norse do not seem to have settled in the Pictish heartland.

What language did the Picts speak?

Contemporaries say that the Picts spoke a different language from their neighbours (the Scots, the Angles and the Britons), and St Columba (a Scot) needed an interpreter when he spoke with them. But we do not know what that language was, and posterity has left us very few examples of it. There are three main sources for the language of the Picts: inscriptions in ogham and Latin letters; a group of names of places; and the names of individuals recorded by writers outside Pictland.

Ogham was a form of writing which originated in Ireland during the first centuries AD; each letter is shown by a group of up to five strokes on a line or the edge of the stone. The scheme may have been based on a five-finger sign language, such as is still used today, where the fingers of one hand in various combinations are laid against the palm of the other. Most of the 36 ogham inscriptions found in Pictland are hard to understand, whichever way up they are read. The Glasgow scholar Katherine Forsyth has shown that many of the ogham inscriptions are in a Celtic language; while the linguist Richard Cox has argued that a number of the inscriptions are in Old Norse. If we go by other inscriptions of the times, in Wales and in Ireland, they ought to represent personal names – even more likely if the stones on which the inscriptions are found can be seen as memorial stones. The few Latin inscriptions, such as those on the Drosten stone or the St Ninian's chape, contain some familiar words but the names can be equally hard to recognise.

At the present time there are in Britain . . . five languages and four nations – English, British, Scots and Picts. Each of these have their own language; but all are united in their study of God's truth by the fifth – Latin – which has become a common medium through the study of the scriptures

Bede

The Brandsbutt Stone, Inverurie, Aberdeenshire
Two stylish symbols – the crescent and V-rod and the snake and Z-rod – are incised on the face of a stone; along the far edge is a line of ogham script, which reads (from bottom to top): IRATADDOARENS. The linguist Richard Cox believes this inscription to be in Old Norse and reads it (from top to bottom) as CQERA OLLAVAR I, which translates as 'Made by Olafr I . . .'.

(*left*)
The Drosten Stone (St Vigeans 1), Angus
This stone carries a worn inscription on its right side which begins: DROSTEN IPE UORET ETT FORCUS.
HISTORIC SCOTLAND

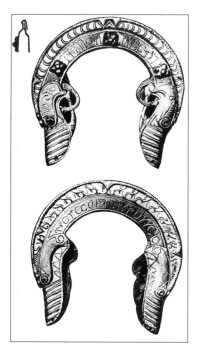

Inscribed 'Sword-chape' from St Ninian's Isle, Shetland

This object carries one of Pictland's rare inscriptions, which has been read 'IN NOMINE D[ei] S[ummi]' on one side, and on the other 'RESAD FILII SPUSSCIO'. Resad and Spusscio could be Pictish names transliterated by an Irish scribe; or Spusscio could be 'spiritus sancti'.

AFTER O'DELL

Some names of Pictish leaders are given in contemporary sources. Bede knew a Bridei son of Mailchon who was the northern Pictish king met by Columba in the 500s, and the southern king Nechtan son of Derile, who adopted the Northumbrian form of Christianity in the early 700s. For other names we have to go to some later medieval documents which are difficult to corroborate. One document says that 29 successive kings of Pictland were called Brude, a word equivalent to Bridei, which seems as though it should relate to Prydein, the Welsh name for Britain. Nine kings are called Drust, which might be the same name as the Drosten which is inscribed on a stone from St Vigeans. The Drosten stone also seems to feature the names Uoret ('Voret') and Fergus, the latter a Scottish name. Other popular names of Pictish kings were Gartnait (at least six of them), and Talorc (at least three). One southern king of the 700s was named after the Roman Emperor 'Constantine'; he was the son of another Fergus, who may have been a Scot.

Adomnán recorded St Columba's meeting with two named Picts:

During the time when St Columba spent a number of days in the province of the Picts, he was preaching the word of life through an interpreter . . . he asked a wizard called Broichan to release an Irish slave-girl, having pity on her as a fellow human-being. But Broichan's heart was hard and unbending, so the saint addressed him thus, saying: 'Know this, Broichan. Know that if you will not free this captive exile before I leave Pictland, you will have very little time to live'. He said this in King Bridei's house in the presence of the king.

An argument about the Pictish language

Expert A: We cannot understand Pictish inscriptions because the Picts spoke a much older language than Celtic or German; it was probably not Indo-European at all, but a survival from the Bronze Age or even earlier, like the language of the Finns or the Basques.

Expert B: The Picts spoke a p-Celtic language, related to British, as the place-names make clear. There was no 'non-Indo-European survival'. The reason that Bede thought Pictish was different from British may have been because the British language had evolved differently either side of Hadrian's Wall.

Expert C: The Picts spoke a p-Celtic language but made increasing use of q-Celtic words as contact with the Scots increased in the 700s, especially since ogham was an Irish method of writing. The personal names belong to a high rank of society where mixing of Britons, Scots and even English people was normal in marriage treaties.

Expert D: The Pictish ogham inscriptions are in Old Norse and commemorate people with Old Norse names. They seem to be quite late, however, perhaps eleventh century (in which case the inscriptions are considerably later than the stones they are marked on).

Where did the Picts come from?

Having no texts written by themselves, the Picts are at the mercy of many theories as to who they were and where they came from. Some believe they were mainly indigenous folk, the descendants of the people who had used the carved stone balls over 2000 years before, and not part of the later Celtic-speaking group which dominated Britain, Ireland and central Europe. This is held to provide the explanation for their apparently unusual customs: their provinces were supposedly inherited through the female line, the new queen taking a male consort for marriage and defence, generally from outside the community.

But, for most modern scholars, the Picts were Britons, just like the Britons of Wales. In this view, there is nothing particularly strange about their customs: they were not matrilinear, they just fell back on female heirs when necessary like the rest of early medieval Europe. Their weapons, forts, social organisation, marriage customs and clothing were not radically different from those of the other communities who occupied Britain and Ireland then. In practice, Irish, British, Anglian and other Scandinavian peoples all no doubt contributed to their ethnic make-up, especially given the likelihood of refugees fleeing from both the south (Britons and Angles) and the west (Irish and Scots). The Picts were not a race, although they may have been briefly a nation.

It is unlikely that new contemporary documents about the Picts will come to light, and our main hope lies in archaeology – the science of understanding people through their settlements, livelihood, burial practice and monuments. This 'material culture', which the Picts imprinted on their land, is slowly coming into focus. Archaeology certainly shows a people who in many ways resembled contemporary warrior-chiefs elsewhere in Celtic and Anglo-Saxon Britain; but in other ways they were distinctive and, whatever the neighbours may have said about them, they had minds of their own.

When the Britons had spread northwards and possessed the greater part of the island, it is said that some Picts from Scythia put to sea in a few longships, and were driven by storms around the coasts of Britain, arriving at length on the north coast of Ireland. The Scots refused them permission to settle so the Picts crossed into Britain and began to settle in the north of the island, since the Britons were in possession of the south. Having no women with them, these Picts asked wives of the Scots, who consented on condition that, when any dispute arose, they should choose a king from the female royal line rather than the male. This custom continues among the Picts to this day.

Bede, around 731

Imprinted on the Land
Memorials and markers: the symbol stones

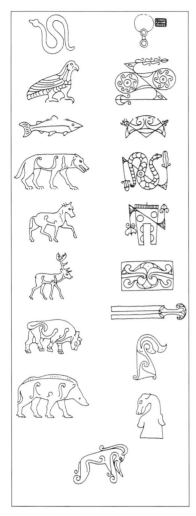

The symbol stones are what makes the lands of eastern Scotland Pictish. The images are unique, graceful and expertly done – but no one knows for sure what they are intended to represent, or why the Picts etched them on metalwork, rocks, cave walls and upright stones.

The symbols fall into two main groups: the ones that consist of animals we can recognise, and which were once native to Scotland; and the ones that are abstract designs. The animals are the snake, the eagle, the fish (a salmon or cod), the wolf, the horse, the red deer, the bull, the cow and the wild boar. The abstract symbols, which have all been given nicknames, are the first group in the picture: at the top is the 'crescent and V-rod', which is also one of the most commonly occurring. A similar kind of broken rod appears again in the form of a Z in combination with a 'double disc', or with a snake, or with a 'notched rectangle', which has been seen as a chariot and horses viewed from above. The floriate rectangle looks like a metal plaque, and the 'tuning fork' reminds one of a sword. The other symbols are the 'flower' the 'dog's head', looking like a glove-puppet, and most famously the 'Pictish beast' dubbed a 'swimming elephant', which has a dolphin-like face and trails a lappet, or long curly piece from its head, like the foam of a wave; but the little tail and wheel-like feet show that it is a composite beast. The mirror and comb are amongst the most easily recognised of the symbols, since the mirror looks just like bronze mirrors found in late Iron Age Britain, for example at Balmaclellan, while the double-sided comb looks just like ones found on Pictish sites.

(above)
A Dictionary of Symbols
From top to bottom: *Left*: snake, eagle, salmon, wolf, horse, stag, bull, boar. *Right*: mirror and comb, double disc and Z-rod ('Z-rod and spectacles'), crescent and V-rod, snake and Z-rod, notched rectangle and Z-rod, rectangle, sword ('tuning fork'), flower, dog's head. *Bottom centre*: Pictish beast ('swimming elephant').
RCAHMS

(right)
The Crescent and V-rod
An ornate example of the 'crescent and V-rod' from the Hilton of Cadboll stone.
NATIONAL MUSEUMS OF SCOTLAND

The ways the symbols are displayed fall into two kinds or classes. In the first kind ('Class I'), which are the earliest, the symbols are incised onto the face of large boulders or slabs. These stones are found all over the eastern lands, generally positioned on the edge of good arable land where it meets the upland. The second kind ('Class II') are done in relief on upright slabs which are cut to a rectangle, sometimes tapering towards the top. The Class II stones carry crosses, scenes from Christian scripture, everyday life and weird composite beasts. They cluster around the Moray Firth and Tayside, two areas which appear to have been strongly targeted by the Christian missions.

Bronze plaque, Monifieth, Angus
A drawing of a bronze plaque from Monifieth, Angus, suggesting that the crescent symbol could have referred to an ornament of dress or hair (like a tiara). This one (and its owner?) was subsequently appropriated by a Viking whose name, Grimkitil, can be seen scratched on it in runes.
NATIONAL MUSEUMS OF SCOTLAND

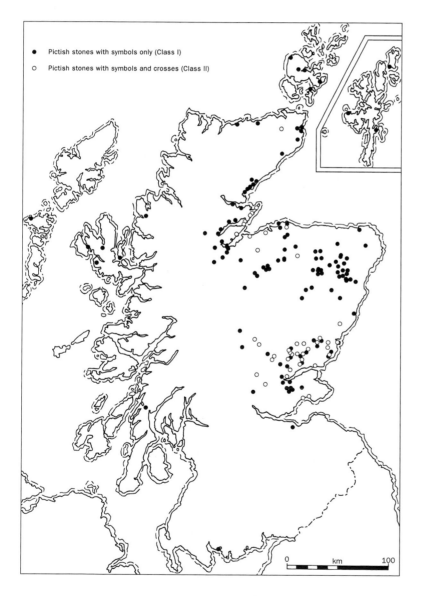

● Pictish stones with symbols only (Class I)

○ Pictish stones with symbols and crosses (Class II)

0   km   100

Distribution of Class I and Class II Stones
The Class I symbol stones are situated in the areas of good arable land. The Class II stones, which also carry Christian motifs, seem to concentrate in the two main Pictish power centres in the Moray Firth and Tayside.

What do the symbols mean?

Archaeologist Charles Thomas saw the symbols as memories of late Iron Age weapons and equipment; perhaps the symbol stones were used instead of placing these things in a grave: a broken spear, a sword, a chariot. By the time the images came to be used by the Picts, in the fifth to seventh centuries, they were symbols of rank, and indicated who was remembered and who set up the memorial. So the Dunrobin stone could mean 'Erected to a Warrior of the salmon-people by his wife'.

The anthropologist Anthony Jackson has suggested that the symbols are records of marriage treaties, typically made on boundaries of united lands, and especially necessary where descent is through the mother. The symbols refer to families or kinship groups which, occurring in pairs and triplets, record the interest that each family retains. The Dunrobin stone (below) might be interpreted as recording a marriage between the salmon and sword families. The mirror and comb indicates that bridewealth was paid by the senior family.

By contrast, the Glasgow scholar Ross Samson looked on the symbols as representing the elements of names; each symbol gives the sound of a Pictish word or syllable, which joined together make up a name. An equivalent in Anglo-Saxon would be Aethel-wulf – loosely 'Noble Wolf' – or Sigebert 'victory bright'. So in this interpretation the Dunrobin stone might mean 'In memory of a woman called Salmon-sword' or more prosaically 'Here lies Mrs Swordfish'.

Other scholars have shown how the stones are likely to mark out territory or land and most agree that the probable function of the symbols is to celebrate a named individual, in line with practice in neighbouring Celtic and German lands.

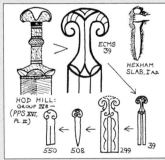

Possible Symbol Sources
(*above*) A late Iron Age mirror from Balmaclellan.
(*below*) A comb from Buckquoy.
NATIONAL MUSEUMS OF SCOTLAND

Decoding the Pictish symbols
The stone depicted is known as Dunrobin 1 and it shows a fish, a 'tuning fork' (perhaps a sword?) and a mirror and comb. Most Pictish symbol-fish are thought to be salmon.
RCAHMS

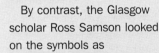

Possible Symbol Meanings
Thomas' derivation of the 'sword' symbol.

What is the date of the symbol stones?

Carving images or patterns on stones is at least as old as the neolithic period, and the Pictish symbols seem to echo Iron Age forms; but the idea of erecting stone monuments was probably learnt from the Romans. The symbols look much the same over a wide area, suggesting a common symbolic language. The symbol stones do not occur in Argyll, traditionally thought to have been settled by Scots from around AD 500, implying that the stones were a later development. However, if the Scottish settlement took place earlier, then the symbol stones could have begun earlier too. The form of the animals on the Pictish stones is close to the animals depicted in the first Insular Gospel books produced in the late 600s, and this has led some to suggest that the Picts' stone carvings started around then, when they had already been exposed to Christianity. But the Pictish symbols are not Christian, and may have been anti-Christian, in meaning.

There are no firm dates, and the story of the Pictish use of symbols is likely to have been long and complex. A beginning between the 400s and 600s is perfectly possible, the symbols being drawn on wood and textiles, or even tatooed on skin, before being transferred to stone. As time went on, the symbols acquired a style which had much in common with art in Ireland and elsewhere in Britain. Monuments bearing symbols on unshaped stones, the so-called 'Class I', were generally superseded by monuments (the so-called 'Class II') which, as well as carrying the symbols of the Picts, also featured those of Christianity. This is thought to have happened following Nechtan's overtures to the Northumbrian Church in 710 and his subsequent expulsion of the Columban clergy (see page 44). The Class II monuments were popular around the power-centres in the Moray Firth and Tayside where the meaning of the crescent and the double-disc remained current alongside the new symbol of the cross. But the erection of Class I monuments could well have continued in areas of less centralised power, like Aberdeenshire. The depiction of solitary animals may also have continued (or even started) later and could have had a different meaning from that of the abstract symbols. One could say that the Pictish symbols were in use from the 400s to the 800s, appearing on unshaped stones during the 600s, and with Christian symbols from the 700s. After about 850, they were apparently never used again, and their meaning was lost.

Burying the dead

During the Iron Age, people in Scotland, as elsewhere in Britain, were buried in a crouched position in pits, examples being found at Broxmouth, in East Lothian. But some time in (or after) the Roman period, the burial rite changed: people were laid on their backs, sometimes in graves lined with stone slabs, the so-called long-cist burials. At the Catstane, Edinburgh Airport, excavations of about fifty of these graves included five cist burials dated by radiocarbon to the 400s or 500s. Excavations at The Hallow Hill near St Andrews revealed 150 cist burials, 19 of which were dated (also by radiocarbon)

to the 600s or 700s. The majority of the cist burials discovered so far cluster in the south-east of the country, and are less common in the regions which featured the Pictish Class I monuments. But this diagnosis may change: long-cists have also been encountered in Orkney, Shetland, Caithness, Sutherland and Easter Ross. There is a theory that the long-cist burial-rite denotes Christianity, and that it arrived in southern Pictland with St Ninian; on this analysis the long-cists further north may prove to be signals of spasmodic and possibly later conversions. But it may be that the long-cist has deeper roots in prehistoric practice, which favoured the use of stone slab linings, and that there is no direct equation with Christianity.

The Garbeg Cemetery

(above)
On the ground at Garbeg, with Loch Ness in the distance. An observer on this spot in the 500s might have seen the boats carrying the missionary St Columba and his party travelling slowly up the Loch to his meeting with the Pictish leader Bridei son of Mailchon.
M.O.H. CARVER

(above right)
The symbol stone found by the landowner Mr John Younie in association with Cairn no 1.
T.E.GREY FOR INVERNESS MUSEUM

(below)
Plan of the cemetery, with round and square grave-settings.
RCAHMS

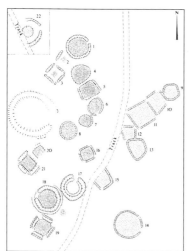

Boysack Mills, Angus
Ploughed-down square barrow under excavation at Boysack Mills, Angus
GORDON BARCLAY

Another signature of Pictish burial recognised in recent years is the use of interrupted ditches around small burial mounds (barrows) formed of earth or stones. The barrows may be round or square in shape and can have a kerb of stones. These cluster around Inverness (for example the cemeteries known at Garbeg and Whitebridge) and Tayside and The Mearns, which puts them in the Pictish zone, but they are still largely undated. Round barrows are found everywhere in Bronze Age Britain, while square ditched barrows are found in Iron Age Yorkshire and France, some famously containing chariots. Square ditched burials have been found in early medieval British areas, such as Wales, but are also known from contemporary Scandinavia.

None of these cemeteries and very few of the mounds have been properly excavated as yet, but we can guess that the square (and round) ditched grave was used during the Roman and Pictish periods. The square ditch at Boysack Mills enclosed a deep grave containing a coffin, in which there was a corroded ring-headed pin which places the burial in the first or second century AD. At Lundin Links, Fife, long-cist burials under cairns have given radiocarbon dates of the 400s to 600s. At Dunrobin an excavated cist grave containing the skeleton of an adult female was dated by radiocarbon to the 500s to 700s. The grave was covered by a rectangular cairn of stones 9.5m by 7m, upon which had originally stood the symbol stone Dunrobin 2. Symbols stones have also been discovered to have been in association with burial mounds at Tillytarmont (Aberdeenshire), Garbeg (Invernessshire), Waternan (Caithness) and Ackergill (Caithness). So, there are now enough cases to lead us to the conclusion that symbol stones were often erected over burials.

Strongholds

In the thousand years before the Romans
came to Britain, the large hill-fort was a
key feature of society: fortified central
places where tribute in the form of food
could be collected and stored, and power
and ritual exercised. After the Roman
Empire had collapsed, forts became
important again in early historic Scotland,
and took several forms. In general they
were smaller and there were many more of
them, implying that society was fragmented
into numerous small lordships. In the west,
small rocky outcrops were fortified – the
duns; in the east, some of the old Iron Age
hill-forts were re-occupied. In the north,
the sites of fortified houses – the *brochs* –
were re-used. To some extent, these
choices were probably determined by the
prehistoric sites and the different terrain and
materials available. If there were hills, these
were fortified and, if there were no hills,
stone fortresses were built or re-used, or enclosures dug.

The Fort of Dundurn
Dundurn at the head of Strathearn.
HISTORIC SCOTLAND

In the Pictish region, only a few strongholds have been
investigated or dated as yet, but we can already identify several
different kinds. In the southern area, Clatchard Craig in Fife enclosed
nearly a hectare with a complex system of ramparts; while Dundurn is
a *dun* or small fortified hillock. There are similar duns all along
Strathearn, which probably indicates a time when this fertile area was
divided between a number of families. Some of these land-holdings
appear to have survived or developed into the historic period where
they are recorded as thanages, or princely estates. On the east coast,
Dunottar is an attractive seaside site, with its beach and rocky
promontory, now occupied by a dramatic later castle. It is also
expected, but not proved, that some of the great Iron Age forts of
Aberdeenshire, such as Bennachie or Tap O' Noth, will have been
re-occupied. Burghead, on the southern shore of the Moray Firth, is a
promontory fort occupied from the 200s to perhaps the 800s. Craig
Phadraig by Inverness was an Iron Age fort recommissioned in the
Pictish period. Still further north, some of the sites of Iron Age brochs
were exploited: houses of Pictish date have been found outside Carn
Liath in Sutherland and Gurness in Orkney. It is not unlikely that
there were also enclosures on lowland sites, fortified with palisades and
earth banks, prehistoric types that were re-used or imitated in the
Early Historic period.

The Promontory of Dunnottar
Dunnottar, south of Aberdeen, has an ideal
combination of an easily fortified
promontory, a beach for landing cargos
brought by sea, and a fertile hinterland.
This is believed to be the *Dun Fother*
recorded in the *Annals of Ulster* as being
under attack in 681. Another candidate for
Dun Fother could be Dinnacaer, an eroded
stack north of Stonehaven where five
symbol stones have been found. The castle
is a much later addition.
M.O.H.CARVER

Four Forts

Craig Phadraig, now on the northern outskirts of Inverness, was an Iron Age vitrified fort, re-occupied in the Early Historic period. In the sixth century, St Columba is thought to have passed up the Great Glen towards the Moray Firth on his mission to the northern Picts. At a certain steep site he met a king, Bridei son of Mailchon, at his fortress and attempted to convert him to Christianity. Craig Phadraig is a favourite candidate for the site of this meeting, and, interestingly, fragments of pottery have been found there, of a type imported from France mainly into Christian countries bordering on the Irish Sea.

> Once, the first time St Columba climbed the steep path to King Bridei's fortress, the king puffed up with royal pride, acted aloofly and would not have the gates of his fortress opened at the first arrival of the blessed man.
>
> Adomnán

(*above*)
Examples of E-ware pottery
These potsherds, from seventh-century France, are of a type which reached Clatchard Craig and Craig Phadraig.
EWAN CAMPBELL

(*facing, right*)
Craig Phadraig Summit
The summit seen from the air in 1994.
RCAHMS

(*right*)
The path to Craig Phadraig
The path winds uphill through the woods and the old ramparts of the vitrified fort to the summit which was re-occupied in Pictish times.
M.O.H.CARVER

(right)

Finds from Pictish Dundurn

(a) A glass boss; (b) metal-working mould;
(c) a silvered bronze 'dangle' with an
animal-shaped terminal; (d) a decorated
leather shoe.

FROM ALCOCK ET AL.

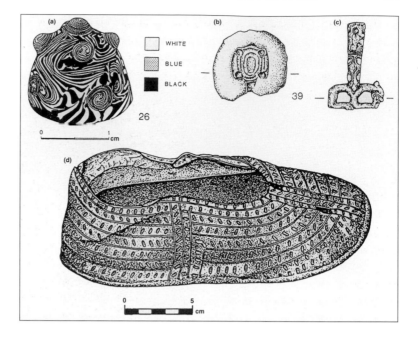

Map of Dundurn

FROM ALCOCK ET AL.

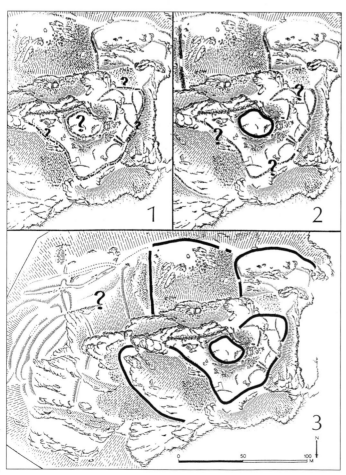

Dundurn is mentioned as being under siege in ad 683 and its imposing mound at the end of Strathearn makes it a natural candidate for investigation. Excavations by Leslie Alcock have shown that it was fortified at least three times during a period dated by radiocarbon to between the 500s and 800s. The earliest fortification had a palisade pegged into a sill-beam anchored in a rock-cut trench. The stockade was then demolished. Later (around the 700s) the citadel was fortified with ramparts built on a framework of large timber beams (200mm square), probably fastened together with iron spikes. In a third phase (around the 800s), following destruction by fire, the ramparts were remade with dumps of rubble. Inside the enclosed summit, wattle and daub and a midden of animal bone show that people were definitely in residence. Finds of a decorated leather shoe, fine metalwork and glass, metalworkers' moulds and a crucible give an exciting preview of a major Pictish power centre.

Burghead. The great promontory fort of Burghead, on the south side of the Moray Firth, is remarkable for its complex defences. The triple rampart cutting off the headland seems to have been built of rubble and may have originally been a promontory fort of the Iron Age, while the curiously shaped double-enclosure on the headland itself is a development of the Pictish period. This inner fort had walls 8m thick, was faced with stone and built on a framework of timbers fastened with iron spikes about 200mm long. In the north-eastern half of the double-fort there is a magnificent well, originally hewn out of the living rock and approached by irregular stone steps. Excavations in the 1800s found buildings inside this enclosure, with an open space by the well.

Burghead is also famous for its very particular symbol stones: at least 30 are mentioned in old records and six have survived, every one carrying the distinctive portrait of a stocky bull, in a style belonging to the 600s. The bulls are incised on slabs of stone which must have been set up as markers inside or outside the fort. In the bend of the bay to the west is an extensive beach which probably acted as Burghead's landing place. Now the site is much altered. Between 1805 and 1809, a new

Burghead from the Air
Burghead in an air photograph taken from the north-west in 1977, showing the nineteenth-century harbour and the planned town.
RCAHMS

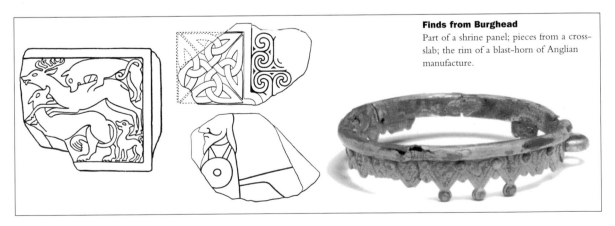

Finds from Burghead
Part of a shrine panel; pieces from a cross-slab; the rim of a blast-horn of Anglian manufacture.

The Burghead Well

The well's gloomy interior calls to mind
pagan rituals and retains something of a
chilling atmosphere. Adomnán of Iona
reported: 'Once when St Columba spent
some time in the land of the Picts, he heard
reports of a well that was famous among the
heathen population. Indeed the foolish people
worshipped it as a god because the devil
clouded their sense.' St Columba sanctified
this well for Christian use, but early Christians
too were highly respectful of the power of
water, and continued to regard many wells in
Scotland as holy places. The Burghead well
has also reminded visitors of the practice of
execution by drowning; a recorded victim
was Talorgen son of Drustan, a king of
Atholl, drowned by Angus son of Fergus in
739. However, the Burghead well was
refashioned in the 1800s. Tunnelled into the
rock, it no doubt followed the line of a
spring, and the construction of a cistern and
steps to approach the water level would have
been a practical measure required to serve the
large community of people and animals
implied by the size of the enclosed area.
HISTORIC SCOTLAND

Inside the Fort at Burghead

At an entrance to the inner
fortress at Burghead in about 800.
The rampart is composed of a
frame of squared oak beams
joined with iron spikes. The wall
is 8m thick. The famous bull
symbol, virtually unique to
Burghead, was incised on panels
of stone. They may have been
arranged as a frieze around the
fort interior, or outside. At the
time depicted, the bull emblems
were up to two centuries old but
were still in place. A war party
returns: the spears and square
shields of the foot soldiers and
the round shields of the mounted
warrior are based on images from
the Class II stones. The fine
sword is composed of the 'tuning
fork' symbol, and its chape from
the St Ninian's Isle hoard.
Around the rider's neck is an
Anglo-Saxon blast horn captured
in some encounter with the
Angles.
MIKE MOORE

(*left*)

Plan and Section of Burghead

This plan was produced
by General Roy in
1793. The part of the
double-enclosure that
lies to the south-west
probably functioned as
the citadel. This part
was quarried away for
the construction of a
deep water harbour in
the early 1800s. The
positions of Burghead
and its neighbours
across the firths –
Dunrobin, Tarbat Ness,
Craig Phadraig
(Inverness) – imply that
the Picts were skilled
sailors in contact with
each other by sea.
SOCIETY OF
ANTIQUARIES OF
SCOTLAND

harbour was built, by cutting a slice off the promontory and building a waterfront, re-using much Pictish masonry.

The churchyard at Burghead was created in the centre of the triple rampart (at 'Church Street'). Eight pieces of decorated stone from the churchyard and around the village, including fragments from a cross-slab, a cross-shaft and a stone shrine, show that there was already an important ecclesiastical establishment here in the 800s. The inner defensive wall seems also to have received attention at that time because a timber from it has been dated to the 800s. Also found at the site and dating to the 800s is a fragment of an Anglo-Saxon decorated blast-horn with a loop for a carrying strap.

Burghead, site of a significant power centre in the heyday of the pagan kingdom of the northern Picts, was thus still a major player in the complex politics of the 800s, in which Scots, English and Norse as well as Picts had an active interest in the fertile lands of the Moray Firth.

The Burghead Bulls
These are two out of six survivors, all found during repairs to the quay or the houses built in the redevelopment of Burghead in the early nineteenth century.
FROM EARLY CHRISTIAN MONUMENTS OF SCOTLAND/ HISTORIC SCOTLAND

RAMPART 1

RAMPART 2

RAMPART 3

RAMPART 4

RAMPART 5

RAMPART 6

The Ramparts of Clatchard Craig
The ramparts as pictured in an air photograph taken in 1932. Excavations and radiocarbon dating show that the fort went through three main phases. In the 400s to 600s, Ramparts 1 and 3 were built on frames of oak timbers; these ramparts were then destroyed by fire. About the 600s, Ramparts 1 and 3 were rebuilt and Ramparts 4–6 added. The fort at this time received pottery imported from France. In the 700s to 800s, Rampart 2 was built, respecting Rampart 1. Inside this smaller fort was a paved hearth, probably marking the site of a rectangular building, and the occupants made penannular brooches.
RCAHMS

Clatchard Craig. Standing on a rocky promontory above the River Tay, the Pictish site of Clatchard Craig has now alas been entirely quarried away. It had probably been in use during the Iron Age and before, but excavations showed that its extant complex of six ramparts belonged to the Pictish period. Finds included imported pottery and glass and clay moulds for making brooches.

Excavations at Clatchard Craig
Excavations across Rampart 2 in progress in 1959.
HISTORIC SCOTLAND

How did the Picts make a living?
What did they eat?

Agriculture was the most important economic activity before the industrial revolution – a full-time job for most and vital for the rest. It can probably be assumed that the Picts farmed Scotland much as people did before and have done since. The native cereals were bere barley and oats. Wheat was probably rare but its cultivation was always possible in many areas of the eastern coastlands, both south and north. Grain was ground with rotary querns, which have been found on sites dated from the Iron Age to the 1800s. Cattle were of paramount importance all over Britain, but especially in the north and west; sheep, of the thin hairy kind, grazed the uplands and produced wool, milk and cheese, and pigs foraged in the woods, occasionally interbreeding with the wild boar. Salmon ran in the rivers and there were shellfish by the shore; sea-fishing was perfectly possible and on the rocky ledges there were gannets' and puffins' eggs. All these we can guess, from what there is now, what was drawn on the symbol stones, and sometimes from the collections of bones and seeds that have so far been found in archaeological work.

The principal goal of human beings is to liberate themselves sufficiently from the daily grind to enjoy the good things of life. And when agriculture produced a surplus, there was an aristocratic class ready to collect it and expend it. Some of the surplus no doubt went to feed the carvers who produced the symbol stones, who could have travelled from lord to local lord. Other surplus went to feed the metal-smiths, another group of important craftsmen. From the metal-smiths came ornamental bridles for horses, weapons and brooches which, with furs and fleeces and flowing cloaks, contrived to make wealthy men and women magnificent in their progress through the straths. Weapons were not only used for warring on the neighbours, but for hunting game, then probably, as for many since, the greatest passion of all. Judging by the pictures on the stones, stag-hunting with hounds was the top-ranking thrill. Other pastimes can be guessed at: board-games, like drafts, were a favourite with most Dark Age peoples. The Picts also painted

Drinking on Horseback
An endearing figure from Invergowrie, Dundee. Drinking from horns, pitchers and bowls no doubt extended beyond the quenching of thirst and found a role, then as now, in providing comfort to the old and supporting the young in social confrontation, ritual and recreation.
NATIONAL MUSEUMS OF SCOTLAND

pebbles, which may have had some role in a game, or were imbued with the magical properties hinted at by Adomnán. Men and women combed their hair, so that they looked good and to remove fleas and nits (the small double-sided comb is still used for this purpose today). Hunting, love-making, parties with cakes and ale: we need not doubt that, then as now, when times were good, life was good, and fun was had.

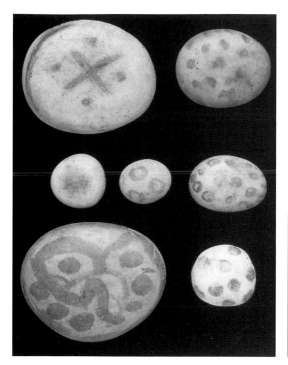

Painted Pebbles from Jarlshof, Shetland, and Keiss, Caithness

According to Adommán of Iona: 'leaving king Bridei's house, St Columba came to the River Ness, where he picked up a white pebble from the river and said to his companions: "Mark this white stone through which the Lord will bring about the healing of many sick people among this heathen race". ...The stone was dipped in some water, where, in defiance of nature, it floated miraculously on the surface of the water like an apple or a nut....The stone was kept in the royal treasury. Whenever it was put into water, it floated and by the Lord's mercy it brought about the healing of many ailments among the people.'

NATIONAL MUSEUMS OF SCOTLAND

Hunting: The Noblest Sport

A party of Pictish aristocrats prepare to go hunting in Strathearn about AD 800. The hounds show that most will be pursuing the red deer, but one lord has been given a hawk by a lady, riding side-saddle. The drinking bowl, as a stirrup cup, is being passed round to steady excited nerves. All the images on the carved stones point to the Picts having had magnificent horses, expertly bred and schooled, and up to 15 hands in height. The wealthy youngster in the foreground shows off her bridle with its silver and niello strap-distributors.

MIKE MOORE

Pictish settlement

Within the forts, and in numerous farmsteads around them, there must have been many houses, but very few have been found and successfully excavated as yet. The type of house favoured in the later Iron Age, round and accompanied by underground storage chambers (souterrains), may have continued in use in early historic times. A new type of turf house, long and thin and round-ended like later Norse houses, has been identified in Perthshire and Angus . In the far north, houses of a similar shape are built of stone slabs, as at the Wag of Forse. In the northern and western islands, the Picts or their contemporaries built 'cellular' houses – a figure of eight as at Buckquoy (Orkney) or Bostaidh (Lewis), or round rooms surrounding a central space, like the 'shamrock' house built originally into the ruins of the Broch of Gurness.

Ploughed-down Settlement of Pitcarmick Type at Lathrisk, Fife
RCAHMS

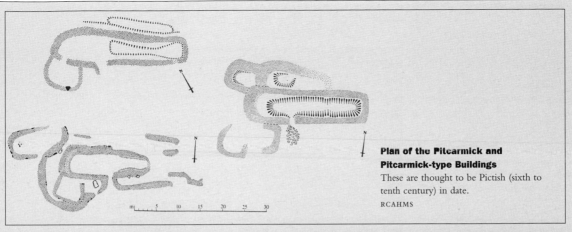

Plan of the Pitcarmick and Pitcarmick-type Buildings
These are thought to be Pictish (sixth to tenth century) in date.
RCAHMS

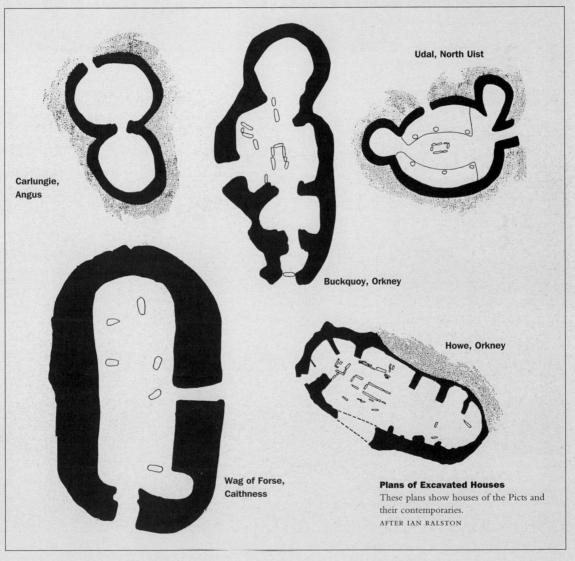

Udal, North Uist

Carlungie, Angus

Buckquoy, Orkney

Howe, Orkney

Wag of Forse, Caithness

Plans of Excavated Houses
These plans show houses of the Picts and their contemporaries.
AFTER IAN RALSTON

Looking good in the sixth century . . .

Early Pictish Accoutrements

(a) Silver bracelet with a diameter of 64 mm from the Gaulcross hoard. (b) Silver chain 279mm long from the Gaulcross hoard. (c) Silver and red enamel pin 143mm long from the Gaulcross hoard. (d) Silver chain 480mm long with Pictish symbols from Whitecleugh. (e) Silver pin from Golspie, 60mm long, with a human head terminal. (f) Silver plaque from Norrie's Law. It is 91mm long and has no obvious means of attachment, so the idea that it could have been an ornamental pendant is purely speculative.

NATIONAL MUSEUMS OF SCOTLAND

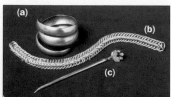

Double-sided Comb and Pins

Comb and pins from excavations at Buckquoy, Orkney. The people seen on the Pictish symbol stones (men and women) had long hair but seem to have kept it neat, using combs and no doubt fastenings of various kinds.

NATIONAL MUSEUMS OF SCOTLAND

An Early Pictish Woman

This woman is wearing the Gaulcross pin and bracelets, and ear pendants like the Norrie's Law plaques. The Norrie's Law hoard was found about 1819 at the foot of Norrie's Law, a prehistoric mound in Fife. On discovery it consisted of 25lb (about 13kg) of silver, but most of this was dispersed and melted down. The Gaulcross hoard was found shortly before 1840 in a stone circle called Gaulcross at Ley in Banffshire. Only three pieces of the hoard now survive. These objects date from the 500s to the 600s.

MIKE MOORE

. . . and in the eighth century

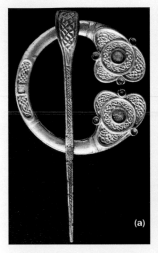

Eighth-century Accoutrements

(a) A silver-gilt penannular brooch from Rogart, Sutherland: 77mm across with trilobe terminals. (b) Silver-gilt brooch-pin (pin 113mm long) found at Dunipace, Stirlingshire, but perhaps made in Ireland. (c) A silver-gilt penannular brooch from St Ninian's Isle, Shetland: 71mm across with snarling beast terminals.

NATIONAL MUSEUMS OF SCOTLAND

A Later Pictish Man

The early Picts seemed to have used handpins to fasten their clothes and worn bracelets; but in the eighth century the penannular brooch was *de rigeur*. This man's cloak is fastened with a penannular brooch similar to those found at St Ninian's Isle and Rogart. The St Ninian's Isle hoard, which included 28 silver objects, was found in 1958 under a stone slab in a ruined medieval church. The Rogart brooches were part of a large hoard largely destroyed found by workmen during the construction of a railway in 1868. The objects date from the later 700s.

MIKE MOORE

Thinking Christian

When, and how – and why – were the Picts converted to Christianity? Christianity brought clear advantages to early medieval leaders, such as a trade network with the other Christian nations and international support for the ruling dynasty; and there were advantages for the people too, such as the protection offered to women and children from the horrors of war enacted in Adomnán's Law of the Innocents. But there were also disadvantages: the church establishment had to be supported either by an extension of taxation or the endowment of land, and Christian rule ran the risk of becoming inflexible and imperious. The expectation is that the Picts would been converted when they encountered missionaries; but this does not necessarily follow. They may have deliberately reserved judgment on what was a crucial political issue.

The people of Pictland were introduced to Christianity on at least three occasions. First, in the 400s, the southern Picts are said to have been converted by Ninian, a Briton who had his headquarters at Whithorn in Galloway. The traces of this conversion may have been left in the form of the long-cist burials and the sculptured stones carrying incised inscriptions or simple crosses in low relief which are found at Whithorn and as far north as Fife. Another clue should be provided by place-names including the element 'eccles' from the Latin *ecclesia*, meaning a church. On the other hand, the stone monuments may be due to late Roman Christians,

The Skeith Stone
This stone is from Kilrenny, north-east Fife.
T.E.GREY

Long-cist Cemetery
This cemetery was excavated at The Hallow Hill, near St Andrews. The long-cists are oriented approximately east by north-east and examples were radiocarbon dated to the seventh to eighth century.
EDWINA PROUDFOOT

rather than those converted by St Ninian; and cist burial may have been a more widespread as well as a more enduring rite.

> *The southern Picts, who live on this [the Northumbrian] side of the mountains, are said to have abandoned the errors of idolatry long before [Columba] and accepted the true Faith through the preaching of Bishop Ninian, a most reverend and holy man of British race, who had been regularly instructed in the mysteries of the Christian Faith in Rome.*

> Bede

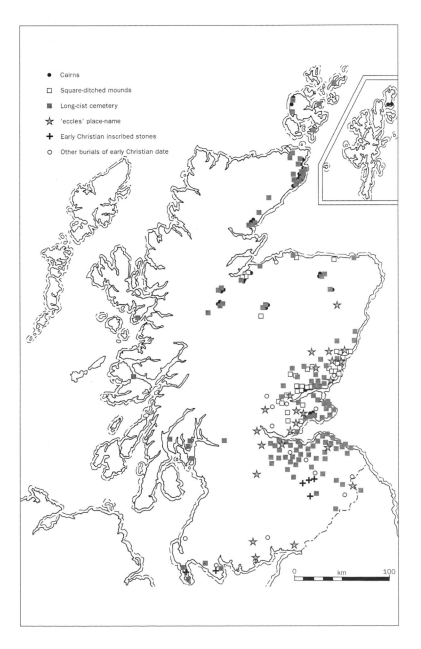

- ● Cairns
- □ Square-ditched mounds
- ■ Long-cist cemetery
- ★ 'eccles' place-name
- + Early Christian inscribed stones
- ○ Other burials of early Christian date

0   km   100

The Catstane in Midlothian
The inscription has been read: IN OC TV MVLO IACIT VETTA F[ilia] VICTI: 'In this mound lies Vetta daughter of Victus'.
HISTORIC SCOTLAND

Christian Progress
Map showing the distribution of early Christian stones, 'eccles' place-names and long-cist burials. Also shown are the locations of early historic barrows and cairns.
AFTER EDWINA PROUDFOOT

The northern Picts were visited by St Columba around AD 565. Columba travelled up Loch Ness by boat, and had the first recorded encounter with the Loch Ness monster. He then met king Bridei at his fortress and engaged in a number of competitions with his wizards. Although Columba won the magic-competition, there is little clear evidence for Christianity in the north at this time. King Bridei's

The Monymusk Reliquary

This is an eighth-century house-shaped shrine for carrying sacred relics. It is thought to be the *Brechennoch* of St Columba, a sacred battle-box used as a rallying focus by the Scottish army. It was associated with military service owed from the lands of Forglen in Banff in the twelfth century and probably earlier.
NATIONAL MUSEUMS OF SCOTLAND

fortress has not been identified: popular candidates are Craig Phadraig, the promontory which now carries Castle Urquhart, and Torvean.

Bede felt that the mission of St Columba had been effective:

In the year of our Lord 565, when Justin the Younger succeeded Justinian and ruled as Emperor of Rome, a priest and abbot named Columba, distinguished by his monastic habit and life, came from Ireland to Britain to preach the word of God in the provinces of the northern Picts . . . Columba arrived in Britain in the ninth year of the reign of the powerful Pictish king Bridei son of Mailchon; he converted that people to the Faith of Christ by his preaching and example, and received from them the island of Iona on which to found a monastery.

Adomnán, who had closer knowledge of Columba, claims only some conversions: 'A Pictish layman heard him [St Columba] and with his entire household believed and was baptized, husband, wife, children and servants'. But he felt that Columba's reach was extensive by the late seventh century when he was writing. Recording two great plagues (probably those of 664 and 680–6), from which both the Scots and the Picts had been spared, he attributed this miraculous escape to St Columba, who 'founded among both peoples the monasteries where today he is still honoured on both sides'.

A third Christian initiative was due to the Northumbrian Angles, who tried to conquer Pictland and impose religious authority on it throughout the later 600s. The conquest failed after the Northumbrian king Ecgfrith was trapped and killed with his army at Nechtansmere (Dunnichen Moss) in 685. But a later Pictish king, Nechtan son of Derile, decided in 710 to align with the Angles after all, and sent for details of the English kind of Christianity, which, among other things, calculated the date of Easter by a different method to the church of Iona. Their monks also used a different tonsure: a circular patch on top of the head instead of a shaven forehead with long hair at the back. Advice arrived in the form of a letter from Ceolfrith, abbot of Wearmouth and Jarrow, which was swiftly promulgated in Pictland. Nechtan subsequently expelled clergy of the Columban persuasion from southern Pictland, but it is unlikely that the Picts turned their backs on Irish Christianity for long, given the named kings reigning jointly over Picts and Scots from the mid 700s. The success of this period of conversion is thought to be

Stones from the Battle of Nechtansmere

(right and facing page)
Dunnichen, Angus. A block of sandstone nearly 5 feet high with a flower symbol, a floriate Z-rod with double disc and the mirror and comb. The stone was said to have been found in 1811 near the marshy ground which has been identified as the site of the Battle of Nechtansmere (Dunnichen Moss) which took place in AD 685 (see frontispiece).
RCAHMS

demonstrated by the great series of
stone monuments, the Class II stones,
which, while still carrying Pictish
symbols, also carry the cross in a
prominent position.

*At this time [about 710] Nechtan, king
of the Picts, living in the northern parts
of Britain, convinced after an assiduous
study of church writings, renounced the
error [the practice of the Celtic Church]
hitherto maintained by his nation about
the observance of Easter, and adopted
the Catholic time of keeping our Lord's
resurrection with all his people. In order
to do this more smoothly and with
greater authority, the king asked for
help from the English people, whom he
knew to have based their practice long
previously on the pattern of the holy,
Roman, apostolic Church. So he sent
messengers to the venerable Ceolfrith,
Abbot of the monastery of the blessed
Apostles Peter and Paul, which . . .
stands at the mouth of the River Wear
. . . The king requested Ceolfrith to
write him a letter of guidance that
would help him refute those who
presumed to keep Easter at the wrong
time . . . In addition, he asked that
architects be sent him in order to build
a stone church for his people in the
Roman style, promising he would dedicate it in honour of the blessed
prince of the Apostles . . .*

Bede

The reverse side of Aberlemno 1 stone,
which is supposed to have recorded the
defeat of the Northumbrian king Ecgfrith
by the Pictish army led by king Bridei son
of Bili. Archaeologist Anna Ritchie has
interpreted the scene: (from top to bottom)
Ecgfrith flees from Bridei son of Bili,
dropping his sword and shield; Ecgfrith
confronts footsoldiers; after facing Bridei,
Ecgfrith is killed and becomes carrion for a
raven. Bede's description of this event,
disastrous for his people, speaks of 'narrow
mountain passes'.
RCAHMS

Ceolfrith duly replied, explaining the Roman rules, in a letter thought
to have been composed by Bede himself, who describes its reception:

*When this letter had been read in the presence of King Nechtan and
many of his more learned men, and carefully translated into their own
tongue by those who could understand it, he is said to have been so
grateful for its guidance that he rose among his assembled chieftains and
fell on his knees, thanking God that he had been accounted worthy to
receive such a gift from England.*

*The new Easter cycles were immediately sent out under a public
order to all the provinces of the Picts to be copied, learned and adopted.*

Whether the English prescription was really welcomed with such raptures we may question. Bede was a Northumbrian Angle, and his account reflected an English viewpoint. Regrettably we have no voice which represents Pictish opinion at such a crucial moment in their history. But the significance of this incident as a change in political direction is clear. There was an issue to resolve and Pictland had resolved it in favour of the perceived allies of St Peter, among whom were the English kingdoms of the east coast. Bede felt that the measure had stuck; at the end of his book he wrote:

> At the present time [AD 731], the Picts have a treaty of peace with the English, and are glad to be united in Catholic peace and truth to the universal church.

How far the Picts had practised organised Christianity before or after this event is hard to say. As yet no certain Pictish books, churches or monasteries are known in Pictland before the 800s, by which time it had become a Scottish territory served by a Scottish church. It may be that the Picts themselves never took to the idea of an established church. Many examples of the Class II monuments, initiated at about the time of Ceolfrith's letter in the early eighth century, now stand in churchyards, but it is not usually known whether the stone was placed beside a church or a church built beside a pre-existing stone.

Converting the Stones

The back and front of Meigle 1 stone, Perthshire. Side 1 is a busy composition featuring a large number of symbols: a salmon, Pictish beast, snake and Z-rod, dog's head, the mirror and comb and a triquetra (a triangular knot). A group of five horsemen and a hound seem to form a hunting party, but an angel hovers in front of one of the riders. A camel-like creature and a coiled snarling beast lurk on the right of the picture. Side 2 is dominated by a cross infilled with interlace pattern; between its arms are a number of beasts which may represent the tamed forces of darkness.
HISTORIC SCOTLAND

Prominent stones were used to mark boundaries, and Class II stones could also have functioned in this manner marking the location of independent estates. Some certainly have complex Christian themes, suggesting a more than superficial knowledge of the scriptures; but examples also featured secular activities like hunting and hawking. Christian images do not necessarily have to be made by monks: the ability of the aristocracy to understand and communicate Christian ideas (as pre-Christian ones) should not be overlooked. Covered with images, personal or ceremonial, these monuments provide a marvellous archive of Pictish activities and ideas.

An argument about the Pictish conversion

Expert A: The peoples of Pictland were converted by Ninian in the fifth century. The conversion began in the south with missions from Whithorn in Lothian and Fife, as shown by the 'eccles' place-names and sculpture of Whithorn type. It later spread to the whole of eastern Scotland and up into the northern isles, as the dedications to St Ninian show. The Pictish church is a British church and traces of this British Christianity will eventually turn up all over the land . . .

Expert B: St Columba's recorded expedition in the sixth century is only the first of many penetrations of the east by the Irish church and people. As Adomnán said, and as the dedications of churches show, Columba founded monasteries in Pictland, and the conversion proceeded steadily from them during the sixth, seventh and eighth centuries. The Pictish church, when found, will resemble the monastic, Scottish church of Iona.

Expert C: The early missions from the British and Irish west were ineffective and there was little organised Christianity in the east and north of Scotland until the early

eighth century. It was then introduced from Northumbria, using Anglian religious art and following the Roman episcopal idiom. The Northumbrian conversion is signalled by the Class II stones, the only evidence for Christian Picts we have.

Expert D: All the churches, whether so-called Celtic or English or British were equally dedicated to Rome and made equal use of Bishops and monks. People did not distinguish between the western and southern churches except in matters of detail, such as the date of Easter and the tonsure. Christianity was gradually acquired by the Picts as they saw the sense in it. There are bound to have been Pictish churches, monasteries and Bishops' seats, both with and without Class II stones; they just haven't been found as yet.

Expert E: It mattered a lot to the Picts whether Christianity was adopted from Ireland and Dál Riata or from Northumbria, since this carried different political implications. The Picts probably treated every Christian overture with equal suspicion, since it threatened their independence. The Class II stones are the monuments of a secular church, retaining authority for the local lords. A centralised and established Christian church came only with Scottish political control in the later eighth century.

Christian Roadside Markers
The cross-slab Aberlemno 3 stands nearly 3m high beside the road leading from Forfar to Brechin. The cross is accompanied by angels bearing books, while on the other face (*facing page*) a hunting scene is topped by an ornate crescent and V-rod and double disc and Z-rod. Among the hunters there are images of the Biblical King David, with harp, rending the jaws of the lion (bottom right) and possibly standing with a square shield on the centre left.
HISTORIC SCOTLAND

St Ninian's Isle: an early Christian centre?

A Selection of Objects from St Ninian's Isle

NATIONAL MUSEUMS OF SCOTLAND

This St Ninian's Isle is not situated in St Ninian's homeland near Whithorn, but off Shetland. And the treasure found there dates not from St Ninian's time, or even St Columba's, but to the later 700s. By this time the people of Shetland, as in the rest of Pictland, had had plentiful exposure to Christianity from both west and south, so that we can expect to find motifs from Ireland, Northumbria and further afield embedded in Pictish Christian practice.

The famous treasure was found in 1958 during the excavation of a ruined medieval chapel. It consisted of 28 silver gilt objects and half the jawbone of a porpoise, which had been placed in a larchwood box and buried beneath a piece of a cross-slab at the east end of the nave. The objects comprise one hanging bowl, seven other bowls, two sword chapes, a sword pommel, a spoon, a hooked implement, three cone-shaped mounts and twelve pennanular brooches. The objects show strong affiliation with eighth-century Northumbrian art and were probably concealed in the church at a time of unrest due to the Vikings in about AD 800. The pommel and chapes must have already been removed from their parent objects before being put in the box, so the hoard could have been that of a metal worker, or even, given that it was covered by a broken cross-slab, of a Viking.

A Christian Burial at Portmahomack, Easter Ross, around AD 785

A man is laid to rest in a cist burial, among the memorials of his colleagues and kin. Memorials with simple crosses probably reflect the influence of Scottish Christianity from Iona and the west coast. The great monumental slab, standing some 3 metres high, is a speciality of ninth-century Easter Ross. The cemetery at Portmahomack stood on a little hill looking out across the Dornoch Firth. It had a sheltered beach which attracted settlers and traders over many thousands of years. The first chapel was probably built in the 800s.
MIKE MOORE

The 'Dragon Stone'

The stone monument found at Portmahomack in 1995. The stone is incomplete and once continued both downwards and to the side. One side features a fabulous beast, a dragon, with its snake's-head tail and part of the cross, infilled with peltaic ornament. The other side shows two lion-like animals confronted over the half-carcass of a deer, with a bear slouching in the top right-hand corner. Below is a row of clerics, some carrying books. These may be intended as monks or evangelists or, given the space available for the figures, as Christ and the apostles.

UNIVERSITY OF YORK

Tarbat – a Pictish monastery?

At Portmahomack on the Tarbat peninsula on the shore of the Dornoch Firth is a beach ideal for landing boats. Beside it stands Tarbat Old Church, the site of a Pictish centre which has produced 36 carved stones belonging to the 700s–800s and featuring a wide range of styles. The earliest burials encountered in the church were long-cist burials, and in the fields beside the church a settlement is being excavated (see page 61). One stone carries a Latin inscription providing a strong hint that this could be the site of a monastery.

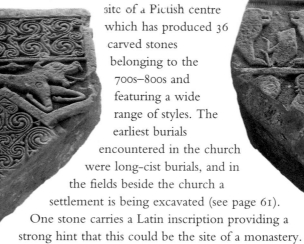

The Carved Stones, Tarbat Old Church, Portmahomack

These stones offer an anthology of memorial styles which look both north and south. (a) There was a cross-slab with a simple cross formed by four circles, which is now lost, but is reminiscent of the western British type which occurs at Whithorn. (b) A grave-marker of a type known from Iona. (c) The base of a decorated slab (Tarbat 1) which carries vine scroll of a type favoured in Northumbria; Pictish symbols are carved in relief on one edge.

IAN SCOTT

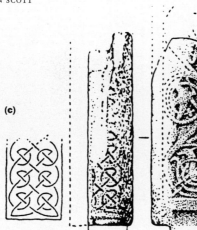

(a)

(b)

(c)

The Hilton of Cadboll: Site and Stone

This famous stone formerly stood at the site of a medieval chapel at Hilton of Cadboll. The earthwork of the ruined chapel is the rectangular shape in the centre at the foot of the photograph.

The Hilton of Cadboll sculpture is now in the National Museum of Scotland. A masterpiece of carving, it features an ornate double-disc and Z-rod, and crescent and V–rod. Below these is a hunting scene, apparently led by a woman riding side-saddle. A plant-scroll with pecking birds forms the border.

BARRI JONES; HISTORIC SCOTLAND

The Tarbat Inscription

This is one of the longest Latin inscriptions known in Pictland. It occurs on part of a memorial stone found in the garden wall of the manse of Tarbat parish church at Portmahomack, Easter Ross. The inscription is done, unusually, in relief and the form of the letters recalls those of insular manuscripts made in the eighth century such as the Lindisfarne Gospels or the Book of Kells. The ornament matches that on a large piece of a stone monument discovered at Portmahomack in 1995, the so-called 'Dragon Stone' seen on page 50.

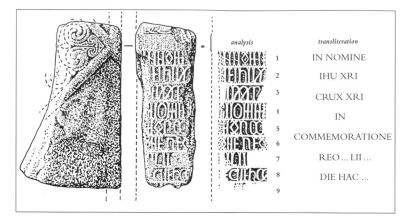

	analysis	transliteration
1		IN NOMINE
2		IHU XRI
3		CRUX XRI
4		IN
5		COMMEMORATIONE
6		
7		REO ... LII ...
8		DIE HAC ...
9		

Making a Pictish Stone

(above right)

Barry Grove carving a replica of Tarbat 1 (see page 50) in low relief in 1998. The pattern was sketched out in pencil on the slab, but the sculptor is producing the pattern by eye. As he does the interlace, he is muttering 'over', 'under' to himself. The piece of stone represents perhaps a fifth of the original monument. But it still took eight people to carry the block from the quarry on the shore to a vehicle (right).

E.R. CARVER; STEVE MILES

Open Air Archive – Windows on Pictish Life and Thought

The Class II stones provide enticing glimpses of Pictish life and thought – but must be used with care. We cannot just read off the activities, because the pictures may have originated somewhere else. This is especially true with pictures of Christian subjects, which must have been copied from books or ornamental carvings depicting people and events a long way from Scotland. So every scene on a Pictish stone has to be systematically checked to see if its images have been 'borrowed' from another culture. All the images on these pages come from carvings made in Pictland in the eighth to ninth century, but some of them may have first occurred in Roman or Byzantine art, or in England, Ireland, France or Scandinavia. The Picts were Europeans and up to date.

Some things, like the hunting scenes, can be accepted as home-grown, and used to evoke the life and ways of the real Picts; and even when exotic or Christian subjects are chosen – that choice is the choice of the Picts and not without interest in itself.

Fighting

There were mounted warriors with spears and round shields, and foot soldiers with spears and shields which might be round or square. The

Fighting

(a) Mounted warrior at Edderton, Easter Ross. (b) Three mounted warriors at Fordoun, Kinc. (c) Mounted warrior and three foot soldiers with round shields at Dull, Perth. (d) Two foot soldiers with square shields fight it out at Shandwick, Easter Ross. (e) Three foot soldiers with square shields at Brough of Birsay. (f) Benvie, Angus, showing shield, spear, bridle and sword.

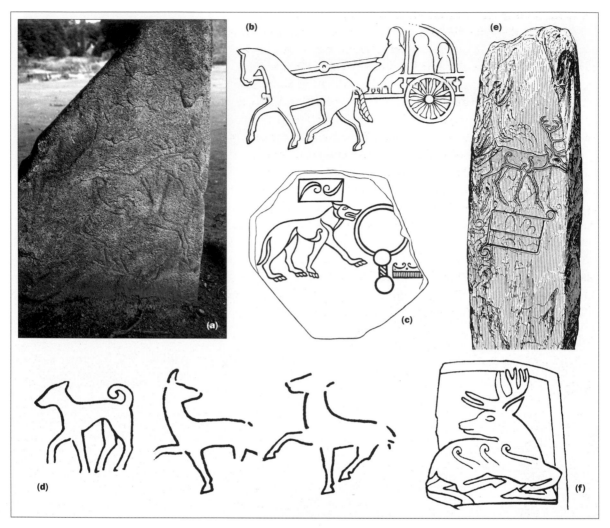

Animals

The picts loved animals: the way they looked and the way they moved. This is clear from the animal drawings on the stones which for their purity of line are arguably unmatched anywhere in the world of art. (a) Horse running free at Inverurie. (b) Meigle 10 (now lost) showed a horse drawing a two-wheel cart. (c) Dog from the stone at Newbigging Leslie, Aberdeen. (d) Dogs from Largo, Fife. (e) Stag at Grantown. (f) Red deer, resting but alert, at St Vigeans.

PHOTO: GORDON BARCLAY

Tarbat Calf Stone

Bucolic scene on Tarbat 28: a family of cattle; it seems to be the father that is licking the new calf.

UNIVERSITY OF YORK/M.O.H.CARVER

square shields may refer to Romans or soldiers pictured in sources from overseas; the round shield is the one featured on the majority of examples, and ought to be a Pictish type. On the other hand, both might have been in use: the round on horseback and the square or rectangular on foot. The small notched shield which appears on the St Andrews sarcophagus and at Ardchattan has a prototype in the Iron Age: miniature examples were found in the Salisbury hoard, and a full-sized one at Deal in Kent. Could the Picts have 'remembered' the form of something last used in the first millennium BC? Certainly – just as techniques for building hillforts or burying the dead were revived in Pictland after an apparent interval of 500 years or more. One day we shall find a real Pictish shield . . . and also perhaps examples of the spears, bows and arrows, which occur in hunting and fighting scenes.

The St Andrews Sarcophagus, Fife
A stunning work of the late eighth century employs the ancient skill of the Pictish carver to celebrate the might of Rome in the style of the new overlords from Irish Scotland. The large figure is identified as the Biblical King David who was a favourite role model for the early medieval potentate: an active leader, fighter and decision-maker, given to regaling the company with his own compositions and beloved of the Almighty.
HISTORIC SCOTLAND

(right)

Hunting Images

(a) A horseman sounds the horn at Dunkeld. (b) Bow and arrow used against a brave stag at Shandwick, Easter Ross.

(below)

Invented Animals

Creatures with hooves, claws and a long-haired human head appear on a stone at Gask, Perth.

Scriptures

Scenes inspired by the Christian scriptures occur from time to time on the stones: King David was the one of the most popular (see p. 55), and other subjects included Samson smiting the Philistines with the jawbone of an ass, Jonah and the Whale and Daniel in the Lions' den. In addition to the meaning conveyed by the scriptures, the selected topics reflected the ethics of heroic society: the gods bless those that survive an ordeal and kings successful in battle.

Curious beasts

On the Christian memorial stones and often beside the cross itself, invented animals may be depicted. With their bits of animal, fish and bird in combination, these curious beasts may have been borrowed from classical stories which came to Pictish ears through Christianity. But the Picts, long experienced in signalling their ideas through animal forms, might simply have made them up. The point of these weird images seems to be to display a message: the beast was like a compound adjective, suggesting bravery, cowardice, triumph or death, an icon of unusual talent or terror, harbingers of good or ill luck. Perhaps heaven was thought to be populated by entertaining or scary images, the equivalent of our 'aliens'.

People and Politics

Were the Picts a tribe, a nation or a kingdom? The question is not yet answered although there is a growing number of clues. The Picts' self-awareness as a people seems to have been first stimulated by the conquest of Roman Britain to the south of them. The feeling of

The Cossins Stone, Angus

This stone, the only one to feature a boat, was probably carved late enough (late eighth to early ninth century), for the boat in question to be Viking. But its six occupants do not look aggressive, and it is reasonable to assume, until we find one, that Pictish ships resembled those of other North Sea peoples.

'otherness' in the people of north-east Scotland, who were not included in the Roman province of Britannia, evolved to a feeling of being a confederacy, as the Roman province began to show its stress in the fourth century. Success in raiding may have led to a clearer sense of identity, not so much a country or a kingdom, as a 'nation' in the sense of the 'Apache Nation'. A uniformity of culture was shown by the stone markers which display common icons from Orkney to Angus. But during the early Pictish period, say the 400s to 500s, we have few obvious hints, in the settlements or the cemeteries, that the Picts had kings.

Through external or internal pressure, societies all over the island of Britain seem to have become markedly more hierarchical in the 600s. In Pictland, many rocky knolls or promontories, some of them sites originally built a thousand years earlier, are fortified, suggesting a number of small lordships. The same kind of social change is evident among the immediate neighbours, the Britons in the south-west, the Angles in the south-east, and the Scots in the west. These three peoples all adopted Christianity during the 600s or earlier, thus openly declaring common cause with the European continent. Even so, their versions of Christianity were not all of the same mould, some preferring the centralisation and regulation of the episcopal system, others aspiring to the virtues of grass-roots monasticism pioneered by the desert fathers, and others again frankly promoting a secular Christianity in the service of local lordship.

These different approaches, none of them either pure or simple, led to confrontation and enmity in which the Picts inevitably participated. We know that the Picts were exposed to Christian missions from their neighbours from the 500s onwards, and the cross appears by the early 700s on the new generation of symbol stones that we call 'Class II'. But the churches and books that are diagnostic of organised Christianity are still lacking. It may be that Pictish Christianity was a more secular affair; enough commitment to understand the message and celebrate it in art, but not so much as to lose control or revenue. The Norse seem to have embraced a Christianity of this kind from the tenth century onwards in both

58 SURVIVING IN SYMBOLS

England and Scotland; thus when Picts and Norse interacted in the north-east and the Northern Isles their encounters may not have been always unfriendly.

From the 700s onwards, southern Pictland became increasingly associated with the Scots, their neighbours to the west, and from an occasionally rough wooing a new political strategy was born. It was one more suited to face the main challenge of a Christian Europe – how to reap the advantages of the continental union without jeopardising independence and sovereignty. The forts did duty into the ninth century, and then became redundant. The new power centres were lowland palace complexes, of which the settlement buried at Forteviot may prove to be an example. The northerners may have cherished a hope of not committing themselves to either the Norse or Scottish camp; but, by the mid ninth century, to stay Pictish seemed to be no longer an option.

What happened to the Picts? In the clash between the Scots and the Norse, the people of the east coast, by now often intermixed and associated by arms and marriage to both, no doubt sided alternately with one and then the other. The Picts did not vanish; they simply became Scots or Norse. Upwardly mobile men and women had to express themselves in Gaelic or Norse, and soon the Pictish language became redundant. Split into many small lordships, without an ecclesiastical establishment, the Picts had no vernacular chronicles with which historians could resurrect their memory through the centuries. Soon only the stones bore witness to the genius of the Pictish era; and then their meaning too was forgotten. It is largely the late twentieth century which has discovered a mission to help the Picts to live again, through the new agenda and methods of art and archaeology.

A Dug-out of the Pictish Period
This dug-out was discovered by salmon-fishers on a sandbank at Errol in the tidal reaches of the River Tay. This kind of craft would be most effective in inland waters.
DUNDEE CITY COUNCIL –
ARTS AND HERITAGE DEPARTMENT

How Will We Find Out More?

Portmahomack and St Colman's Church

The old church of St Colman is the white building standing in its graveyard by the road (top left). A more ancient enclosure surrounding the church was discovered from the air in 1984 by Barri Jones and Ian Keiller during their survey of the Moray Firth area. The site now being investigated lies within this enclosure; occupied throughout the Pictish era, it consisted of a group of buildings on the raised ground above the beach, and seems to have functioned at different stages of its development as a stronghold, a monastery and a beachmarket. The modern village in the foreground is Portmahomack, the 'port of St Colman'.

BARRI JONES

There is so much more to discover about the Picts and eastern Scotland in early Historic times: how did the people live? How and why did they change their style of living? What became of them? The answers to many of these questions lie buried in the ground, in settlements and monuments and objects which are occasionally spotted from the air or tumbled to the surface by the plough.

Rediscovering the Picts is only a matter of time, because the archaeology of Scotland is sympathetcially managed and served by Historic Scotland, by the Royal Commission, by the Council for Scottish Archaeology and by the residents of Scotland themselves. Most casual discoveries get into *Discovery and Excavation in Scotland*, the annual report of what has been found each year. As the discoveries are made, the picture builds up and gets easier to understand.

In harmony with this careful management, research projects are launched each year, targeted on special problems. New art-historical

work on the meaning of the symbol stones, their date and the
activities depicted on them is more or less continuous. New
archaeological field-work has to take its opportunities, but one or two
major projects are usually under way, and can sometimes be visited. At
the time of writing, there is one at *Pitcarmick* in Perthshire where a
new kind of building was identified as probably of the Pictish period
by survey work in 1990, and excavation has confirmed that the houses
and the settlement belong to the late first millennium.

The political story of the northerners, how they measured up to
the challenges of their day and dealt with the attentions of their
neighbours to the west, east and south, are being studied in the *Tarbat
Discovery Programme*, a large-scale archaeological project centred on a
site at Portmahomack on Tarbat Ness, Easter Ross (see opposite page).
The new sites like Tarbat are located by searching the land from the
surface or from the air, and in selected cases excavation may follow.
Then traces of buildings, burials, artefacts, animal bones and plant
remains are brought to light, all of which helps to answer the
questions: 'what sort of people were these? How did they live? What
did they believe in?'

Other important archaeological projects are under way all over
mainland Scotland and in the Western and Northern Isles, as well as
in Ireland and in neighbouring countries on the shores of the North
Sea. All are in pursuit of new knowledge and understanding about this
pivotal time in Europe's history: that moment when the Picts and
their contemporaries first encountered the ideas of Christianity and
began to express themselves as independent 'nations'. These were
ideas that were destined to last a thousand years.

Sites around Scotland

The main legacy of the Picts consists of hundreds of carved stones, most carrying symbols, many still standing in the open air. There are a number of excellent 'trails' but nothing quite beats the excitement of trying to find the stone you want to see, armed only with Allen and Anderson's *Early Christian Monuments of Scotland* and a map. Listed here are some of the principal collections of stones and visitable sites. At the sites of forts, cemeteries and settlements there is often nothing clearly Pictish to see, but there is plenty of atmosphere.

South

Aberlemno has three famous stones in the open air – two by the road and one in the churchyard.
Dundurn and Strathearn. A ramble along this valley will be repaid by beautiful scenery and a number of intriguing hill-forts, culminating in Dundurn itself.

Sueno's Stone
The stone in its protective box pictured at night.
HISTORIC SCOTLAND

At *Meigle* and *St Vigeans* (by Arbroath) are two of the most important exhibitions of Christian-period stones.
The *National Museum of Scotland* has many of the finest pieces of Pictish metalwork and carving in its care. Much Pictish material is now distributed within the prehistoric 'themed' display in the basement.

Centre

Archaeolink at Oyne in Aberdeenshire is a display centre designed to show off and explain aspects of the past, including the Pictish period. A short walk or drive brings you to a stunning view of Bennachie, with the Rhynie stone below it.
The *Maiden Stone* also lies a short distance from Bennachie.
Sueno's stone stands at Forres, now protected by a large transparent box.
Burghead is a modern township, but traces of the rampart still show. The well can be visited and two of the famous Bull stones can be seen in the Public Library there. Another can be seen in the fine Museum at *Elgin*.

North

Craig Phadraig is owned by the Forestry Commission and a 20 minute walk up the foot path from a car park on the north side of Inverness brings you to its summit. The Iron Age rampart is still visible and lumps of vitrified rampart lie about in the trees.

Groam House is a museum specially dedicated to the Picts at Rosemarkie on the Black Isle. The exhibition includes Rosemarkie's own intriguing collection of Christian Pictish sculpture. The Groam House Lectures form a highly successful series featuring the latest findings and interpretations. Copies of the lectures given so far may be bought from the museum.
A Pictish Trail around *Easter Ross* concentrates mainly on the great monuments on Tarbat Ness: Nigg, Shandwick, Portmahomack. At Hilton of Cadboll, a replica of the famous stone (exhibited in the National Museum in Edinburgh) is being erected.
Portmahomack is a port of call on the trail and also site of the Tarbat Discovery Centre. As well as exhibiting the 36 pieces of sculpture so far found at the site, the display describes a major archaeological research project in search of the northern Picts.
The summerhouse at *Dunrobin Castle* contains one of the most important collections of Pictish sculpture in the country, relating to both the pagan and Christian periods.
Orkney is an archaeological paradise. A famous Pictish stone stands on the *Brough of Birsay*, and artefacts of the Pictish period can be seen in the Museum at *Kirkwall*.

Further Reading

- Adomnan of Iona *Life of St Columba*, edited and translated by R. Sharpe (Penguin 1995)
- *The Early Christian Monuments of Scotland*, by J. R. Allen and J. Anderson (1903, reprinted by Pinkfoot Press 1993)
- Bede *A History of the English Church and People*, edited and translated by L. Sherley-Price (Penguin 1968)
- *The Language of the Ogam Inscriptions of Scotland*, by Richard Cox (University of Aberdeen 1999)
- *Scotland in Dark Age Europe*, edited by Barbara Crawford (St Andrews 1994)
- *Scotland in Dark Age Britain*, edited by Barbara Crawford (St Andrews 1996)
- *Conversion and Christianity in the North Sea World*, by Barbara Crawford (St Andrews 1998)
- *Scotland. Environment and Archaeology 8000 BC–AD 1000*, edited by Kevin Edwards and Ian Ralston (Wiley 1997)
- *Language in Pictland*, by Katherine Forsyth (Studia Hameliana 2, 1997)
- *Picts, Gaels and Scots*, by Sally Foster (Historic Scotland/Batsford 1996)
- *The St Andrews Sarcophagus. A Pictish Masterpiece and its International Connections*, edited by Sally Foster (Four Courts Press 1998)
- *Pictish Studies*, edited by J. G. P. Friell and W.G. Watson (BAR 125, 1984)
- *The Picts*, by Isabel Henderson (Thames and Hudson 1967)
- *The Worm, the Germ and the Thorn. Pictish and Related Studies Presented to Isabel Henderson*, edited by David Henry (Pinkfoot Press 1997)
- *A Pictish Panorama*, edited by Eric Nicoll (Pinkfoot Press 1995)
- *Picts*, by Anna Ritchie (HMSO 1989)
- *Pictish Symbol Stones: An Illustrated Gazetteer* (RCAHMS 1999)
- *Scotland. Archaeology and Early History*, by Anna Ritchie and Graham Ritchie (Edinburgh University Press 1991)
- *Warlords and Holy Men*, by Alfred Smyth (Edinburgh University Press 1984)

Acknowledgements

My thanks to Gordon Barclay for inviting me to contribute to the series, and to Mairi Sutherland for editing. I am very grateful to Sally Foster, Alex Woolf and Katherine Forsyth for their often successful attempts to save me from error and moderate my vision. Thanks also to my Tarbat co-directors Justin Garner-Lahire and Annette Roe, and most especially to Emma Carver who did the picture research and provided help and advice at every stage.

Thanks are due to the following individuals and organisations for their permission to reproduce copyright illustrations: Historic Scotland; The Royal Commission on the Ancient and Historical Monuments of Scotland (RCAHMS); National Museums of Scotland; Professor Barri Jones, University of Manchester; Gordon Barclay; T. E. Grey; The University of York; E. R. Carver; Steve Miles; Edwina Proudfoot (St Andrews Heritage Services); McManus Gallery, Dundee; Ewan Campbell; Society of Antiquaries of Scotland.

HISTORIC ⌂ SCOTLAND

HISTORIC SCOTLAND safeguards Scotland's built heritage, including its archaeology, and promotes its understanding and enjoyment on behalf of the Secretary of State for Scotland. It undertakes a programme of 'rescue archaeology', from which many of the results are published in this book series.

Scotland has a wealth of ancient monuments and historic buildings, ranging from prehistoric tombs and settlements to remains from the Second World War, and HISTORIC SCOTLAND gives legal protection to the most important, guarding them against damaging changes or destruction. HISTORIC SCOTLAND gives grants and advice to the owners and occupiers of these sites and buildings.

HISTORIC SCOTLAND has a membership scheme which allows access to properties in its care, as well as other benefits.
For information, contact:
0131 668 8999.

The Pictish Arts Society was founded in 1988 to affirm the importance of Pictish culture. It has regular meetings, and a journal, and is based at 27 George Square, Edinburgh EH8 9LD.

Endpiece

The Pictish picture-stones have attracted some wonderfully ingenious explanations. This interpretation of the Glamis stone comes from Thomas Pennant's *A Tour in Scotland* (1776):

In the churchyard of Glamis is a stone similar to those at Aberlemno. This is supposed to have been erected in memory of the assassination of King Malcolm, and is called his grave stone. On one front is a cross; on the upper part is some wild beast, and opposite to it a centaur; beneath, in one compartment, is the head of a wolf; these animals denoting the barbarity of the conspirators; in another compartment are two persons shaking hands; in their other hands is a battle-axe: perhaps these are represented in the act of confederacy. On the opposite front of the stone are represented an eel and another fish. This alludes to the fate of the murderers, who, as soon as they had committed the horrid act, fled. The roads were at that time covered in snow; they lost the path, and went on to the lake of Forfar, which happened to be frozen over, but not sufficiently strong to bear their weight: the ice broke, and they all perished miserably.

Glamis Stone
HISTORIC SCOTLAND